The Battle of Cantigny

CORNERSTONES OF FREEDOM

SECOND SERIES

Tom McGowen

Children's Press®
A Division of Scholastic Inc.
New York • Toronto • London • Auckland • Sydney
Mexico City • New Delhi • Hong Kong
Danbury, Connecticut

In memory of my uncle, Dorance Nelson, a soldier in the American Army in World War I

Library of Congress Cataloging-in-Publication Data

McGowen, Tom.
  The Battle of Cantigny/Tom McGowen
      p. cm. — (Cornerstones of freedom)
  Includes bibliographical references and index.
    ISBN 0-516-22264-3
    1. Cantigny, Battle of, 1918—Juvenile literature. 2. United States.
Army. Infantry Division, 1st—History—20th century—Juvenile literature.
3. World War, 1914-1918—Regimental histories—United States—Juve-
nile literature. [1. Cantigny, Battle of, 1918. 2. World War, 1914-1918—
Campaigns.] I. Title. II. Series.

D545.C273 M34 2002
940.54'1273—dc21
                                    2001017092

1 2 3 4 5 6 7 8 9 10 R 11 10 09 08 07 06 05 04 03 02

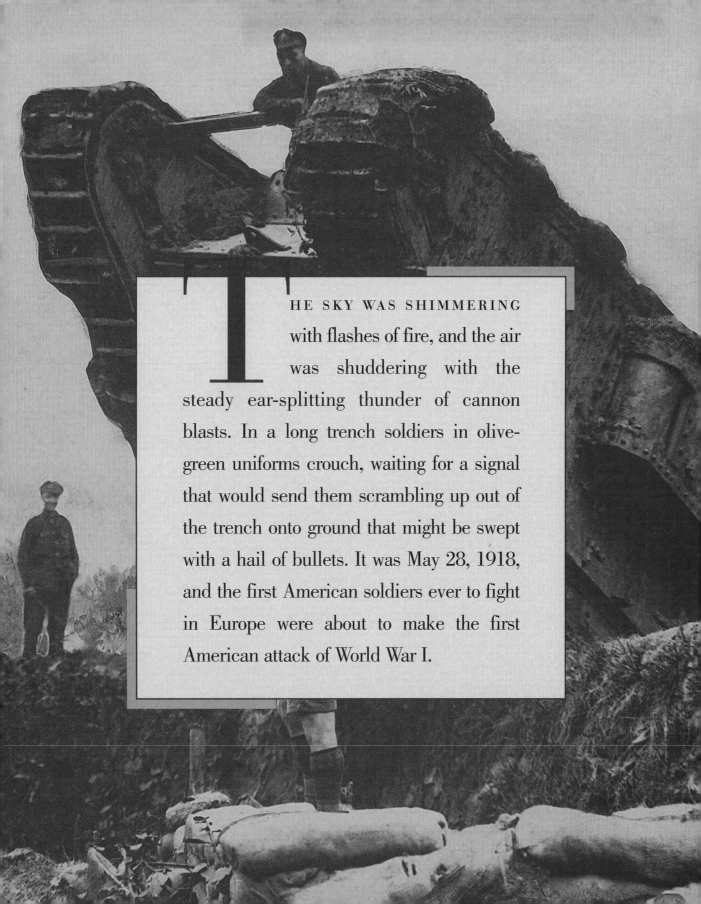

THE SKY WAS SHIMMERING with flashes of fire, and the air was shuddering with the steady ear-splitting thunder of cannon blasts. In a long trench soldiers in olive-green uniforms crouch, waiting for a signal that would send them scrambling up out of the trench onto ground that might be swept with a hail of bullets. It was May 28, 1918, and the first American soldiers ever to fight in Europe were about to make the first American attack of World War I.

* * * *

A WORLD DIVIDED

The war that was to become known as World War I broke out in Europe in 1914. On one side were the Allies—the British Empire (England, Scotland, Wales, Ireland, Canada, Australia, New Zealand, India, and a number of others), France, Russia, and Belgium. On the other side were the Central

British troops arrive in France in 1914 to help the French.

French soldiers during the Battle of the Marne

Powers—the German Empire (encompassing what is now Germany, parts of Poland, and part of France) and the Austrian Empire (Austria, Hungary, Yugoslavia, part of Poland, and some small Baltic nations.)

In Western Europe the war began with the invasion of Belgium and France by German **armies**. A small British army came to France to help the French. The Germans pushed hundreds of miles into France. They were finally stopped in a huge five-day battle near the Marne River. Pulling back, the Germans began digging a long line of trenches—deep ditches in which soldiers could stand and shoot at enemy troops while protected from return fire by the wall of earth in front of them. The French and British

These trenches were dug in the Champagne region of France.

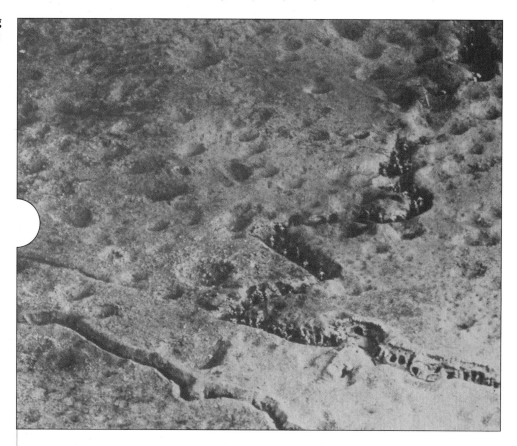

troops quickly began digging trenches of their own. Soon, two rows of trenches faced each other, zigzagging some four hundred miles through Belgium and France.

A DEADLOCKED WAR

On October 29, 1914, the Turkish Empire sided with the Central Powers. The Kingdom of Italy became one of the Allies and on May 23, 1915, declared war on Austria-Hungary. The war became a deadlock, with neither side able to break through the other's line of trenches.

* * * *

On April 6, 1917, the United States, mainly because of the torpedoing of some American ships by German submarines, declared war on Germany and entered World War I on the side of the Allies.

A CRIME THAT HAS STAGGERED HUMANITY: THE TORPEDOING OF THE LUSITANIA

The *Lusitania* sinks after being hit by German torpedoes.

Woodrow Wilson, president of the United States

WORLD LEADERS IN 1917

The U.S. president was Woodrow Wilson. King George V ruled Britain. The president of France was Raymond Poincaré. Germany was ruled by a kaiser (emperor), Wilhelm II; Austria, by Kaiser Karl I; and Italy, by King Victor Emmanuel III.

By this time the British and French armies were in bad shape. They had taken immense losses since the beginning of the war, and they were worn down and dispirited. There had even been revolts in the French army, with troops refusing orders to go into battle. Thus, the British and French were counting on the Americans to come in with fresh troops who were willing to fight.

Wilhelm II, German emperor

Americans fighting in front line trenches during World War I

The German army, too, was in poor condition after years of fighting. German leaders feared the arrival of American troops in France because their forces would then be greatly outnumbered. The Germans decided they somehow had to achieve a great victory over the French and British forces before the Americans entered the action.

Among the very first American soldiers to arrive in France was the man who commanded all the American troops, General John Pershing, with his **staff**. There were about 177 men altogether. They arrived on June 13, 1917.

Americans felt they were paying France back for the help it had given America in the Revolutionary War. The French nobleman Marquis de Lafayette had been a general in the American army and an honored hero in America. Soon after

Pershing and his staff arrived, they attended a special ceremony at a statue of Lafayette, and one of Pershing's staff officers, speaking in French, made the proud statement, "Lafayette, we are here!"

Fifteen days after Pershing's arrival, on June 28, the first American troops, twelve thousand infantrymen of the U.S. 1st Division, arrived. All over the United States, men enlisted to go fight the war in Europe. They were organized into four units, called regiments, of

COMMANDER OF THE AMERICAN EXPEDITIONARY FORCE

General Pershing was officially commander of the American Expeditionary Force, or AEF. American Expeditionary Force was the official name for the entire U.S. Army force in France.

General John Pershing arriving in France

A portrait of the Marquis de Lafayette

Infantry of the First Division resting by a roadside after being relieved of duty in the trenches

around three thousand men each: the 16th, 18th, 26th, and 28th U.S. **Infantry** Regiments. These men wore uniforms of a color officially known as olive drab, or the color of a green olive. Their jackets had high, tight collars, their pants were tight-fitting, and their legs from knee to ankle were covered by canvas leggings that buttoned down the side. They wore broad-rimmed hats that somewhat resembled the hats of cowboys.

The American soldiers who went to France were nick-named doughboys. It is not known exactly where this nick-name came from. It may have been given to them because most of the American army had served on the Mexican border before World War I and were often covered with a

An American doughboy dressed in uniform and throwing a grenade

dry dust typical of that area. This dust was called adobe (ah-doh-bay). Soldiers were first known as adobes, a name that got shortened to dobes (doh-bays) and then might have become doughboys. However the name got started, throughout World War I, American soldiers were called doughboys.

American cavalry on the Mexican border, 1916

Pancho Villa

WHY WAS THE U.S. ARMY ON THE MEXICAN BORDER?

In 1916, Mexican bandit leader Pancho Villa raided the U.S. town of Columbus, New Mexico, with a small army. Soldiers of the U.S. Army were sent into Mexico to capture Villa, but were unable to find him.

AN UNPREPARED ARMY

Few of the doughboys who came to France in June 1917 had ever been in military combat. The American army was poorly prepared to fight a war. For several years European soldiers on both sides of the conflict had been wearing steel helmets. The helmets protected their heads from the rain of bullets that whizzed through the air when a cannon shell exploded. The American army had no helmets. They were hastily equipped with British helmets, which resembled a soup bowl. From the British they also got **hand grenades**,

American soldiers were introduced to two new pieces of war equipment—steel helmets and automatic weapons.

The French Chauchat was an automatic weapon.

called Mills bombs, which looked like small pineapples. Nor did the Americans have **automatic rifles**, which fire a stream of bullets like a machine gun and are indispensable to an army. They were therefore equipped with French Chauchats, a kind of submachine gun capable of firing twenty rounds of ammunition without stopping. It was not a very good weapon, since it jammed easily and would quit firing. The Americans claimed, jokingly, that it was made from rusty sardine cans. The American army did not have enough cannons, so they were given French cannons, known as French 75s because the width of the barrels was 75 millimeters (3 inches).

The condition of the American army worried the British and the French. The Americans were going to have to fight German troops who were not only extremely well equipped but also skilled and experienced in combat. They knew all

A French 75 field gun and an ammunition cart at the Western Front during World War I

WHY WAS THE U.S ARMY UNPREPARED FOR WAR?

In 1917, America was not yet a great power. Americans didn't believe they needed a modern army, so Congress wouldn't provide money for such things as helmets and automatic rifles. Thus, when America went to war, the army was unprepared.

the tricks and methods of catching an enemy by surprise and causing the largest number of **casualties** possible. How would the inexperienced, ill-equipped Americans stand up to this? The British and French did not think they could. What they wanted to do was place small numbers of Americans in veteran British and French units that could teach them how to survive and deal with the onslaught of German **shock troops**.

When he heard this proposal, General Pershing absolutely refused to consider it. This was an *American* army he told the Allied commanders, and it was going to fight as an *American* army, not as part of the British and French armies.

* * * *

LEARNING ABOUT WAR

The doughboys now began to train for war. They learned how to use their rifles efficiently. The rifles were "bolt action," with a knobbed lever called a bolt sticking out of the right side. After a man pulled the trigger, he lifted the bolt up and to the left, which opened up the breech and caused the empty cartridge to flip out. Then the bolt was pushed back to the right and down, closing the breech and pushing a new cartridge, with a bullet in it, into place. If a soldier did this quickly and smoothly, he could fire as many as fifteen bullets a minute.

The soldiers learned how to throw a hand grenade correctly, how to put on and adjust a gas mask, and how to use machine guns. Artillerymen learned how to use cannons.

An artillery crew at work in the field

This factory worker is filling shells with shrapnel.

Firing a 75 required a number of actions—setting the shell's fuse, slamming the shell into the breech (the bottom of the barrel), closing the breech, checking the sight, and yanking the cord called a lanyard. The American gunners got so good at this, they boasted that they could have one shell in the gun and three others going through the air at the same time.

A World War I cannon fired two kinds of ammunition. The ammunition was called a shell because it was a hollow metal shell filled with an explosive powder. One kind of shell, called shrapnel, was filled with hundreds of bullets. The shell had a fuse that was set to make it explode after being fired from the cannon. When it went a certain distance, the shell would explode in a burst of smoke, hurling the bullets forward in a cone-shaped pattern. A second kind of shell simply hit the ground and exploded with a tremendous burst that could blow a building apart or kill anyone within about twenty yards of the explosion. This was known as a high explosive shell.

THE GERMAN MARCH

On March 21, 1918, German forces suddenly launched an attack that smashed through the British army units in front of them. They moved forward 40 miles (64 km) in four days, until they were only 55 miles (88.5 km) from Paris,

Winston Churchill, who became prime minister of Britain in 1940, speaks at a munitions factory while standing behind explosive shells.

the capital of France. Then the Germans stopped to gather strength. Their leading units were now located in a tiny French village called Cantigny.

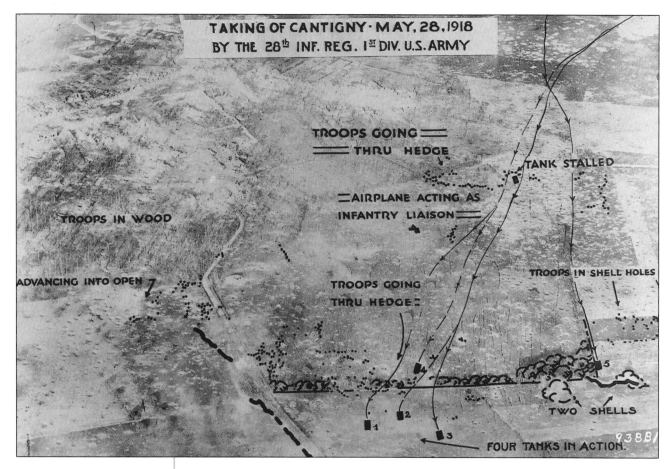

A map of the troop movement through Cantigny

THE SMALL BUT IMPORTANT VILLAGE OF CANTIGNY

Cantigny (kon te NYEE) was the sort of place that is often described as a sleepy little village. It had been home to no more than two hundred people, all of whom had fled before the Germans arrived. Because it was built on high ground, Cantigny provided a good view of the surrounding country-side. That made it valuable to the Germans. In patches of woods behind Cantigny, groups of German cannons were hidden. German **observers** in the town, scanning the countryside through field binoculars, could tell the German artillerymen exactly where to shoot.

About six miles (10 km) beyond Cantigny was a railroad that ran directly to Paris. If the Germans could push forward and capture this railroad, it would be a terrible threat to the Allied forces. The French Army would be split, and the divisions would be unable to speedily come to each other's aid. The Germans would be able to make a quick attack on Paris that might actually force the French to surrender.

It was a dangerous situation for the Allies, and General Pershing knew he had to help. He went to the French commander, Marshal Ferdi-nand Foch, and told him he was willing to have American divisions put in place to help prevent any further German advances. The French marshal instantly requested that an American division be sent to the Cantigny area.

French Supreme Allied Commander Marshal Ferdinand Foch

★ ★ ★ ★

Major General Robert Lee Bullard, commander of the U.S. 1st Division

THE BIG RED ONE

By this time the U.S. 1st Division had been fully formed under the command of Major General Robert L. Bullard. The men had been given their official division emblem, which was worn on the left shoulder of their uniform. It was (and still is today, more than eighty years later) a large red numeral one on a brown background. The division soon became known as "the Big Red One." General Pershing believed the 1st Division was ready for combat and ordered it to go to German-held Cantigny.

An American division was about twice as big as a French, British, or German division. It was composed of four regiments of riflemen, around 12,000 men; three regiments of artillery of almost 5,000 men and 48 cannons; and more than 1,000 men with 120 machine guns. The division also included engineers, who built roads and bridges; wagon drivers, who drove the vehicles containing supplies and ammunition; and others, who took care of various needs. Its total strength was about 28,000 men.

The 1st Division was in position near a little village called Seicheprey. It moved out to head for Cantigny on April 4. The U.S. 26th Division, which was known as the Yankee Division because all its men came from New England, took its place. While the 1st Division was on its way to Cantigny, the German commanders decided to find out how well American troops could fight. On the morning of April 20, after a sudden fierce artillery **bombardment**, 3,200 skilled and experienced German shock troops hit the area around Seicheprey and captured it from the 26th Division. The Americans rallied and made a **counterattack**, and the Germans slipped out of the town. The Americans regained the town, but it was not a victory. The 26th Division had killed only 160 Germans, whereas the Americans had suffered 643 casualties and 136 Americans had been

"The Big Red One" emblem worn by the U.S. 1st Division

WOMEN IN THE WAR

Women were not allowed in any of the U.S. Armed Forces in World War I. However, there were women nurses, telephone operators, and Red Cross workers, who helped care for wounded and did jobs that aided the war effort.

Nurses at a Red Cross hospital during World War I

taken prisoner. The Americans had shown they had courage, but they hadn't shown they could outfight experienced German soldiers.

THE FIRST DIVISION AT CANTIGNY

The 1st Division went into the trenches facing Cantigny on April 24. The Germans knew the Americans had arrived and immediately "welcomed" them with a vicious artillery **barrage** of shrapnel and mustard gas. Mustard gas was a horrible weapon that got its name because it smelled like a combination of mustard and horseradish.

When a mustard shell exploded, it released a cloud of gas that crept forward along the ground. Any soldier who did not get his gas mask on in time began to choke and gasp for breath. His eyes swelled shut, so that he became blind. Even if a man had a gas mask on, the gas might

Hand-to-hand combat during a gas attack

GAS—A HORRIBLE WEAPON!

World War I was the first and last war in which poison gas was used as a weapon. It was such a horrible weapon that after the war the nations of the world voted to forbid its use ever again.

penetrate his clothing, making his skin blister with large painful sores. The men of the 1st Division who were exposed to mustard gas had to be led out of the trenches and taken to hospitals where they could be treated for its terrible effects.

But there were still plenty of 1st Division troops left that could be useful, and General Pershing felt he had to show the British and French that Americans could outfight German soldiers. Again Pershing went to Foch. "Let us make an offensive against Cantigny," Pershing requested. Foch agreed, thinking this offensive might be useful for drawing the Germans' attention away from preparations his troops were making for an attack.

In military terms an offensive is a large, carefully planned attack intended to push enemy troops out of a particular place. Often, troops were specially trained

British Commander-in-Chief Douglas Haig, who led Great Britain's armed forces in World War I.

for offensives, and the 1st Division was given special training for the attack on Cantigny. It was pulled back some distance from Cantigny, to a location where the landscape was very much the same, and where trenches, exactly like those manned by the Germans at Cantigny, had been dug. French officers who were experienced combat **veterans** taught the Americans how to move quickly through such a

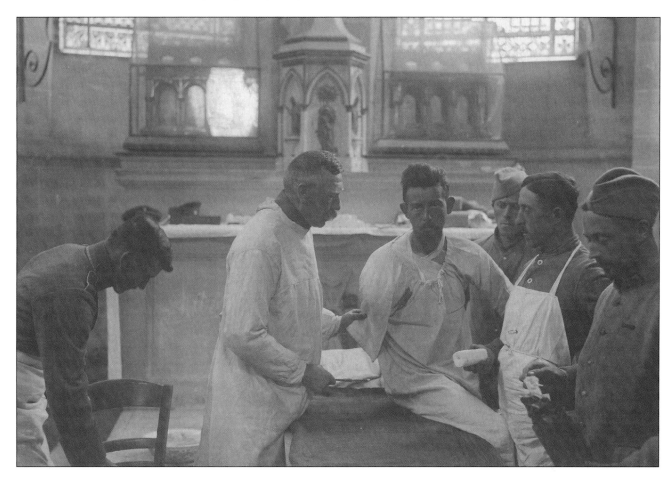

A World War I hospital, where wounded soldiers were taken to be treated.

landscape. They also showed the Americans how to choose the best way to move toward the town, the best places to hide while they fired at the enemy, and how to attack the trenches so they would have the fewest casualties. These were things that inexperienced soldiers who had never been in combat didn't know, and trying to launch an attack without this knowledge could have resulted in enormous casualties.

KEEPING THE SECRET
OF THE BIG OFFENSIVE

When the men of the 1st Division returned to their position in the trenches some distance from Cantigny, the Germans knew it. In an effort to find out what was going on, they made **raids** to capture prisoners they could question. The raids began early on the morning of May 27, with a fierce artillery bombardment on the position of the Second Battalion of the 28th regiment. Then, at about 6:00 A.M., groups of German infantrymen came charging into the American line. The doughboys wiped out many of them with rifle fire and met those who got close enough in hand-to-hand combat with bayonets. A bayonet is the long sword-like knife on the end of a rifle, designed to be rammed into a man's body. In the artillery shelling and hand-to-hand fighting, the battalion lost twenty-one men killed and thirty-nine wounded, but killed forty-eight Germans and drove the rest off.

The Germans did get some prisoners, but these men were killed by machine gun fire as they were being taken to the German lines, so the Germans learned nothing from them. The Americans took three German prisoners, and these men gave their captors a great deal of information. They had been told the Americans were "green," or inexperienced, troops that would probably crumble in the face of an attack, and had expected most of them to run away and others to surrender. They indicated surprise that the Americans fought so well. This made the Americans realize that the

Soldiers charge out of the trenches with their bayonets ready.

German troops in Cantigny would not be expecting a strong attack and could be taken by surprise. They also learned there were no German tanks in Cantigny, which was very encouraging news.

The artillery cannon was one of the most important and effective weapons used during World War I.

THE BIG RED ONE GOES ON THE ATTACK

After the raids, German commanders still didn't know what the Americans planned to do. However, they certainly didn't think it would be an offensive. They felt sure the Americans weren't capable of that.

At about 5:45 A.M. on the morning of May 28, they learned differently. There was a sudden ear-shattering roar of 26 cannons—the 1st Division's 48 guns, plus 178 more that the French army had lent them. An American officer in an observation post described the artillery fire in a report as "great clouds of smoke rolling up from the shelled districts, against which the flashes of bursting shells stood out." The first American offensive was under way.

✶　✶　✶　✶

In the American trenches the noise was so great that the men could not hear themselves talk—or even shout. The thunder of artillery went on for a full hour as shells saturated the area around Cantigny. Then officers, who had been staring at their wristwatches, began waving the men "over the top" and out of the trenches. They gathered into precise formations of three lines, or "waves," spread across a length of one mile. As they began to move forward the pattern of the artillery fire changed. A wall of artillery shells was coming down about 110 yards (100 m) in front of them, creating a line of explosions a mile (1.6 km) long. Every two minutes this line of explosions jumped forward another 110 yards as the sweating gunners, firing twenty-five shells a minute, changed the range. This was known as a rolling barrage. It enabled troops to move steadily forward without any enemy troops being able to come at them through the wall of moving explosions.

Soldiers advance from the trenches.

THE ADVANCE ON CANTIGNY

The first wave of the advance was the 28th Infantry Regiment, its three **battalions** moving in a row, one beside another. The doughboys kept up a steady walking pace. It would have been difficult for them to run because they were heavily burdened. Packs, known as long packs, were strapped to their backs. Long packs hung from the shoulders to below the waist and contained a blanket, a spare pair of shoes, an aluminum **mess kit,** and cans of food. A long spade was stuck through one of the belts holding the pack on, and beneath the pack, slung over one shoulder, was a bandolier, a belt holding a row of pockets full of rifle cartridges. Hanging on each man's chest was a canvas bag containing a gas mask. Most of the men were further weighted down with several

These men carry their supplies in long packs strapped to their backs.

A gas mask, a trench knife, and a water bottle were some of the equipment soldiers carried with them.

hand grenades, a grenade that could be shot from a rifle, a vicious weapon called a trench knife, and two water bottles.

Most of these men moving through the smoky, thundering darkness were frightened—some more than others. But some men were excited by what was happening around them, excited to be part of an adventure. And some men were impassive, simply doing what they had to do, without any excitement or much fear. Whether frightened, excited, or impassive, the men of the 28th Regiment of the 1st Division kept moving forward, toward their objective.

A flamethrower is used in the field.

In addition to their own division artillery, the Americans were receiving help from the artillery of French divisions that were in trenches on either side of theirs. Altogether, 368 guns were pounding the Germans in and around Cantigny.

The French were also helping in other ways. Overhead, flights of French fighter planes circled above the doughboys, protecting them from attack by German fighters. On the ground, a dozen little French Renault tanks were clattering along with the 28th Regiment's battalions, and each company of the 28th had some French flamethrower units with it. The French soldiers were in light grayish-blue uniforms with long, knee-length coats, and strips of cloth called puttees wound around their legs.

Soldiers carried flamethrowers strapped to their backs. The flamethrower was simply an oil-filled tank with an attached hose that ran under a man's arm to a nozzle he held in his hands. With a twist of his wrist, the man could send a flaming stream of burning oil jetting out of the nozzle for a distance of 25 to 40 yards (23 to 36 meters). It was a horrible, frightening weapon.

* * * *

THE BATTLE FOR CANTIGNY

Cantigny was in ruins. It had been shot to pieces by both German and Allied artillery. As the Americans reached the edge of the town, their artillery bombardment instantly stopped so that none of them would be hit. The doughboys entered Cantigny.

TANKS—A NEW WEAPON

World War I was the first war in which tanks were used. They were invented by the British. To keep them secret, they were first called "tanks" in hopes the enemy would think they were just tanks to hold water.

A British tank going over a trench

★　★　★　★

THE AMERICAN SOLDIER'S WEAPON

The weapon of most American infantrymen was a rifle. It could fire five shots, one at a time, before having to be reloaded. A rifle bullet could travel a distance of about 1 ¼ miles (2 km).

The town was full of German troops in their gray-green uniforms, with helmets that resembled old-fashioned coal buckets. They were hidden in houses, in cellars, and behind barricades in the streets. The doughboys started cleaning them out. They shot down anyone who fired at them in the streets, and they threw grenades into houses where they thought enemy soldiers might be hiding. The French flamethrower units spurted fiery blasts into cellars. This generally brought German soldiers scrambling out with their hands in the air. But some came out in flames, dying in agony. German machine gunners behind barricades fired as long as they could and then raised their hands in surrender. The doughboys, who had just seen their comrades shot down, often shot the Germans instead of taking them prisoner.

Eventually, there were no German soldiers left in the town. They had either run away, been taken prisoner, or been killed. Cantigny had been captured by the Americans—only 35 minutes after they entered the town!

A World War I infantryman's rifle, shown here with the five rounds it was capable of firing and a bayonet fixed at the end of the barrel.

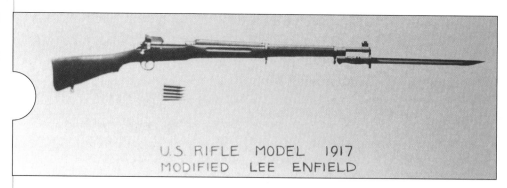

U.S. RIFLE MODEL 1917
MODIFIED LEE ENFIELD

★　★　★　★

Passing through the town, the 28ᵗʰ Regiment stopped beyond it and began digging a trench. General Bullard and the other commanders, knowing that the Germans would eventually make a counterattack to try to recapture Cantigny, wanted the doughboys to have protection.

THE GERMAN ARMY STRIKES BACK

At first, the German commanders didn't know that Cantigny had been captured. They weren't sure what was going on and sent troops to find out. This was not a counterattack, but just fifty men looking for information. As the German soldiers appeared, the Americans threw down their spades, picked up their rifles, and opened fire. The German troops sent to find out what was going on were nearly all wiped out.

It was now about 9:00 A.M., and the German commanders still didn't know what had happened. They sent another small force of about one hundred men to find out. These men, too, were just about all killed by Americans firing Chauchats from the trenches.

When the surviving Germans got back to their commanders, the officers finally understood that Cantigny was firmly in enemy hands. Immediately they began organizing a counterattack. They didn't think they would have any trouble recapturing the town. They believed that it must have been captured by French troops and that the Americans had just

Barbed wire was a major obstacle in trench warfare.

been put in position to defend it. They still thought the Americans were green troops who wouldn't be able to stand up to a counterattack.

The German troops picked to make the counterattack were the 271st and 272nd Reserve Infantry Regiments. They were not the best German regiments. Reserve regiments were second-rate units that were usually put only in defensive positions. They were made up of older men, some in their fifties, and young boys in their middle teens. These troops were not at all eager to make an attack, but they were used to obeying their officers in any situation. Now ordered forward against the Americans, they went slowly and reluctantly.

FIGHTING OFF
THE COUNTERATTACK

The American 28th Infantry had now been reinforced by a rifle battalion of the 26th Regiment and the machine gun companies of the 16th and 18th Regiments. Barbed wire had been strung out in front of the American trenches.

It took a long time for the Germans to get all their attacking troops together. It was 5:30 in the afternoon when the German troops began approaching the American trenches. They carried pipe bombs for blowing their way through the barbed wire, and they were preceded by a rolling barrage from small cannons known as mortars. From the woods around Cantigny, German artillery began firing, pounding the American trenches.

The Americans opened up with rifle fire, Chauchats, machine guns, and mortars. The first line of German troops was literally torn to shreds. From behind the trenches, the 1st Division artillery began a barrage. The second and third waves of German troops were caught in a hail of shrapnel. They broke and began to run to the rear. The counterattack was over.

But the American 28th Regiment had taken heavy casualties, too. Its trenches had been blown full of shell holes from the German artillery bombardment. The 28th's commander, Colonel Hanson Ely, sent the message, "Front line pounded to hell—and—gone," and said he needed **reinforcements** badly.

THE 1ST DIVISION FIGHTS ON

Night fell, and things got quiet. But the Germans did not intend to give up. They planned another counterattack for the next day.

At about sundown the next day, German artillery opened up with a barrage of high explosive shells and

Colonel Hanson E. Ely (center), officers of the 28th Regiment, and a French officer (second from the right)

38

The American victory at Cantigny prevented the Germans from capturing the railroad to Paris.

mustard gas. Three more waves of German infantry attacked the American trenches and were beaten back. But now the 28th Regiment was in a desperate situation. During the night of May 30, they were pulled back, and a fresh regiment, the 16th, was put into the trenches.

On the third day, the Americans again experienced German artillery fire. But gradually it died away. The Germans had given up. No more counterattacks were attempted. The Battle of Cantigny was over, and the Americans had won. The 1st Division had 868 men wounded, 199 killed. German losses were around 1,400 killed and wounded, and 200 had been taken prisoner.

AMERICA SHOWS ITS STRENGTH

Compared to many of the huge, hard-fought offensives of World War I, the Battle of Cantigny was rather small, yet it really had tremendous significance. For the Germans, it was a shock. These inexperienced American soldiers that German generals had thought would be so easy to defeat had turned out to be as brave and tough as the best German troops. This was cause for worry, since soon German armies would be facing hundreds of thousands of these men.

For the French and British, the outcome of Cantigny was reason for joyful celebration. They now knew for sure that the Americans could be counted on. With the large American force on their side, the Allies were certain they would finally win the war.

As for the Americans, they had gained confidence. They had captured the place they'd been sent to capture, and they had held it for three days against everything the Germans could throw at them. They had told the Germans, "Americans can fight—look out!"

Less than six months after Cantigny and after gigantic battles in which hundreds of thousands of American troops were involved, Germany surrendered, and World War I came to an end.

American and French troops comb the battle area after their capture of Cantigny.

Glossary

armies—fighting forces of six or more divisions plus supporting troops, generally totaling 100,000 to 160,000 men

automatic rifle—a weapon that can be carried by a single soldier, which quickly fires many bullets in rapid succession

barrage—a steady fire of artillery shells that forms a long line of explosions to screen and protect troops

battalions—units that make up a regiment. Battalions are generally formed of four companies of 250 men each, for a total of 1,000 men

bombardment—a large number of artillery shells fired into a particular area to cause maximum casualties and destruction

casualties—those killed and wounded during a battle

counterattack—an assault made as soon as possible against an enemy that has just completed an attack in order to regain any ground the enemy has taken

hand grenades—small bombs that can be thrown by a soldier

Infantry—soldiers who fight on foot

mess kit—a small set of cooking and eating utensils used by soldiers and campers

observer—a soldier in an advanced (far forward) position or high place who is able to see what enemy troops are doing over a wide area

raid—a minor attack by a small group of soldiers for the purpose of gaining information or taking prisoners

reinforcements—additional troops or weapons supplied to provide extra strength to a military unit

shock troops—soldiers who are trained and equipped to attack an enemy suddenly and violently, inflicting many casualties and large-scale destruction

staff—a group of officers who assist with the administration of a military organization

veterans—members of a military organization who are experienced in combat

Timeline: The Battle of

1914

JULY 28
Austria declares war on Serbia, beginning World War I.

AUGUST 3
Germany declares war on France. Fighting begins in Western Europe.

1917

OCTOBER 29
Turkey sides with the Central Powers.

APRIL 6
The United States declares war on Germany.

JUNE 13
General John Pershing, commander of U.S. forces, arrives in France.

JUNE 28
The first U.S. Army troops, four infantry regiments of the 1st Division, arrive in France.

Cantigny

MARCH 21
A German offensive pushes forward 40 miles (64 km), its leading units occupying the village of Cantigny.

APRIL 4
The U.S. 1st Division leaves Seicheprey for the Cantigny area. Its place is taken by the U.S. 26th Division.

APRIL 20
The Germans launch an attack on the 26th Division, inflicting 643 casualties and taking 136 prisoners.

APRIL 24
The 1st Division takes up a position in trenches facing Cantigny.

MAY 28
The first American offensive of the war begins. 1st Division troops capture Cantigny. In the late afternoon the Germans launch a counter-attack in an attempt to recapture the town. The Americans defeat it.

MAY 29
The Germans make another attempt to retake Cantigny. Again, the Americans defeat it.

MAY 31
German commander gives up attempts to recapture Cantigny. Cantigny is a clear American victory.

NOVEMBER 11
Germany surrenders. World War I is over.

To Find Out More

BOOKS

Cooper, Michael L. *Hell Fighters: African-American Soldiers in World War I.* Birmingham, AL: Lodestar, 1997.

Hatt, Christine. *World War I: 1914–18.* Danbury, CT: Franklin Watts, 2001.

Kent, Zachary. *World War I: "The War to End All Wars."* Berkeley Heights, NJ: Enslow Publishers, Inc., 1994.

Rice, Earle. *The Battle of Belleau Wood.* San Diego: Lucent Books, 1996.

Stewart, Gail B. *Weapons of War.* San Diego: Lucent Books, 2001.

ONLINE SITES

World War I, The Great War, The Western Front
http://www.rockingham.k12.va.us/EMS/WWI/WWI.html

World War I
www.worldwar1.com/maproom.htm

Index

Bold numbers indicate illustrations.

About the Author

Tom McGowen is a children's book author with a special interest in military history, on which he has written ten previous books. His most recent book in the Cornerstones of Freedom Series was *The Battle of Midway.* Born in the decade after World War I, he grew up in an era when books, movies, and mementos of the war were widespread, and he became deeply interested in it. Later, he served in the U.S. Navy during the final year of World War II. Author of fifty-six fiction and non-fiction books for young readers, he was the 1990 winner of the Children's Reading Round Table Annual Award for Outstanding Contributions to the Field of Children's Literature.